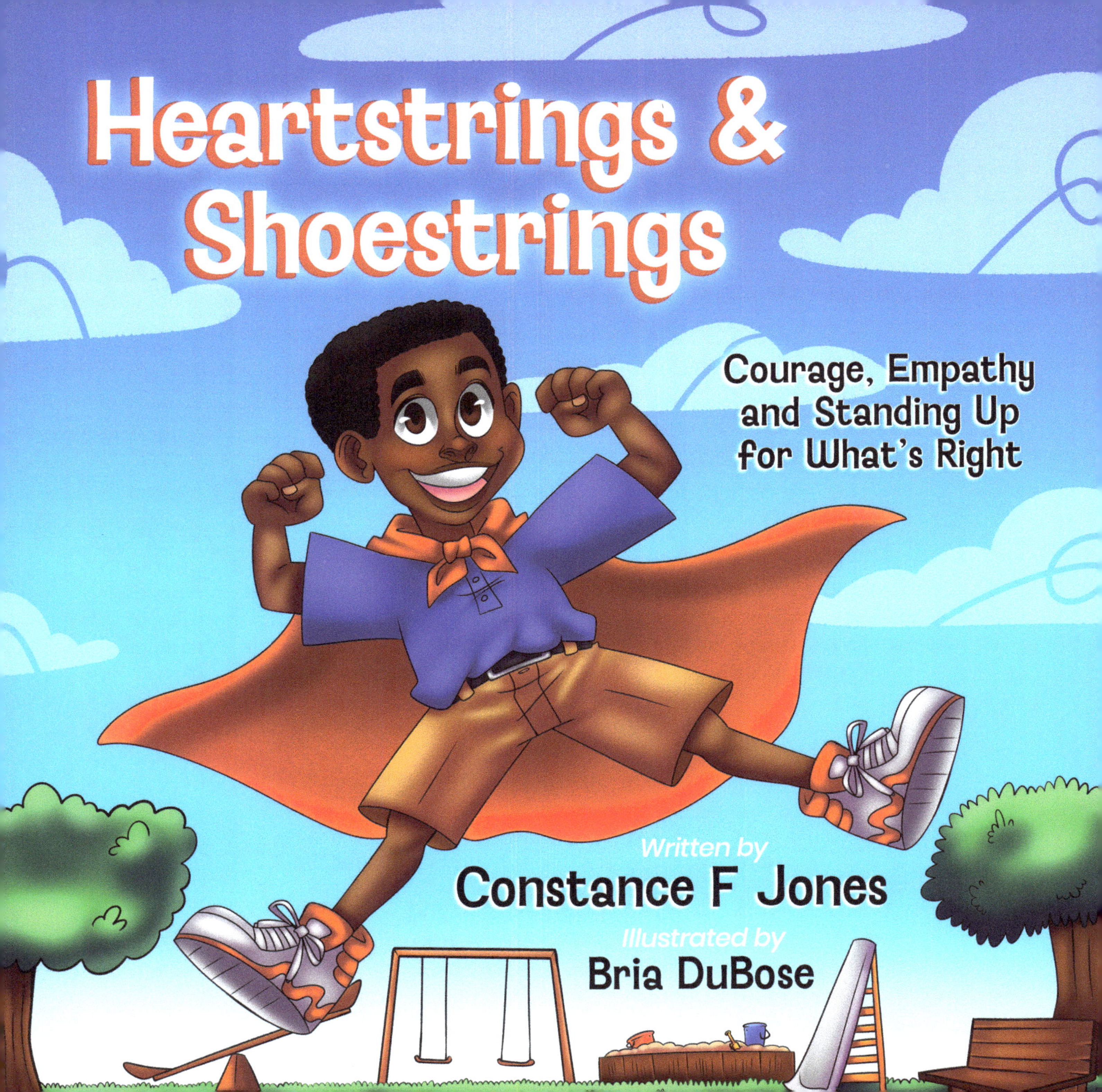

Heartstrings & Shoestrings
Courage, Empathy and Standing Up for What's Right
Written by
Constance F Jones
Illustrated by
Bria DuBose

Hardcover: 979-8-9850903-9-0
Ebook: 979-8-9850903-8-3

Library of Congress Control Number: 2023911350

Illustrations by Bria DuBose
Edited by: Laura Boffa
Compiler: Maria Johnson
Published by: Good Ventures, LLC

You opened the door and invited me inside.
Your gifts for me I share with pride.
My joy and gratitude I cannot hide.
I thank you Father for all that you provide.

Once a Year
BIG SALE
In the blink of an eye,
summer was done.
The back-to-school prep
had officially begun.

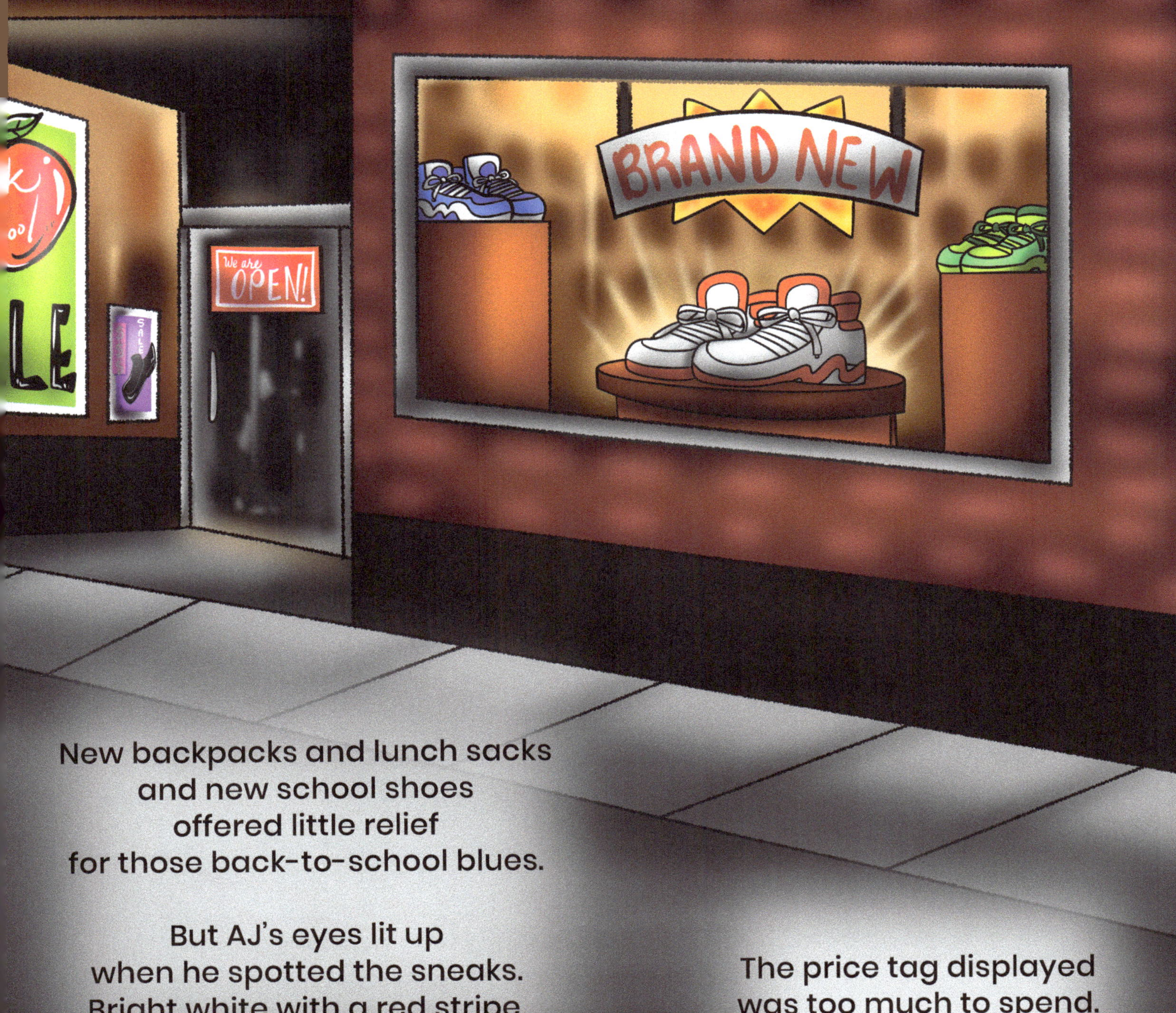

New backpacks and lunch sacks
and new school shoes
offered little relief
for those back-to-school blues.

But AJ's eyes lit up
when he spotted the sneaks.
Bright white with a red stripe,
they were unique.

The price tag displayed
was too much to spend.
He begged and pleaded.
Mom finally gave in.

As the first day of school
played in AJ's head,
his anticipation grew
for the good and the bad.

He remembered hanging with friends,
laughing more than they should.
He remembered the schoolwork.
He'd learned as much as he could.

Now he was ready
for all the first day would bring.
He admired his new cut,
his fresh kicks, and new things.

He walked in with purpose.
He walked in with pride.
He looked good and felt good,
and it showed in his stride.

Suddenly,
Kohen, Will and Candace stood near.
They were pointing and laughing,
but their words were clear.

They stared at AJ's shoes.
Will asked, "What are those?"
These words stung
all the way down to his toes.

And again they laughed
and asked, "What are those?"
AJ wondered, "What's wrong
with the shoes I chose?"

Embarrassed for the attention
to the shoes on his feet,
his spirit was wounded
as he walked to his seat.

AJ felt stuck.
He could not run or hide.
Recess came and went.
He didn't even go outside.

Later at home,
his dad asked why.
"What's wrong, AJ?
You have worry in your eye."

He began to tell his parents
what happened and when.
As he replayed the kids' words,
he felt anxious all over again.

"They pointed and laughed
'cause my shoes weren't the same.
I had no words.
I felt so ashamed."

Mom wore her worry.
Dad wondered what to say
as he watched AJ experience
the burden of the day.

It was time to teach AJ
where courage can be found.
Grabbing the remote,
his dad turned off the sound.

"You have a superpower
hidden inside.
It's silent and still,
just along for the ride."

"A superpower?"
AJ responded. "Who me?
I'm just a kid.
How could that be?"

"It can't be found
in your hands or your feet.
But in your heart and your head,
anytime that they meet.

It's packed up like a parachute,
ready to use.
It sparks quickly like fireworks
when lit with a fuse.

Courage is what we call it,
and it is sure to appear
when we hurt from our feelings
or when fearing our fears.

Courage reminds you
that you are brave and strong.
Listen to your head and heart.
Courage always tags along."

"I need the shoes,
The ones they all wear.
The pointing and laughing
is more than I can bear."

"AJ, remember you are loved
through the skin and to the bone.
You like what you like.
Your style is your own."

His dad wiped the tear
from AJ's cheek.
He reminded him love is stronger
than the likes you seek.

AJ walked his new shoes
into class the next day.
He carried his confidence and courage,
ready for what they had to say.

But there was no pointing
or laughing like the day before.
They all just ignored him
and the shoes that he wore.

But on the playground at recess,
it started again.
And this time, they taunted Kaylin
and Raylin, her twin.

Their words were hurtful,
ugly, nasty and poor.
Each word just as painful
as the one before.

Kaylin and Raylin moved quickly,
far away from the drama.
But what happened next
would bring them
both trauma.

A pebble struck Raylin
just above her eye.
She stood frozen in fear,
and she started to cry.

The pebbles and the tears,
they continued to flow
as other kids stood by
and just watched the show.

All of a sudden,
AJ heard his dad's voice.
Then his heart and his head
made the clear choice.

His courage lit up
like fireworks at night,
and he led them to safety.
He did what was right.

The twins were so grateful.
The teacher took action.
Bullying was no longer
the main attraction.

AJ's head filled with purpose.
His heart filled with pride.
He did good. He felt good.
And it brought back his stride.

At home, AJ explained
What had happened and why.
His dad called him a hero.
Mom tried not to cry.

"Son, empathy and courage
are like best friends.
They help each other.
And then everyone wins."